START QUILTING

with

ALEX ANDERSON

Six Projects for First-Time Quilters

C&T PUBLISHING

Thumbs up to all quiltmakers about to be born.
May your journey be filled with creative joy
and new friendships.

CONTENTS

© 1997 Alex Anderson

Developmental Editor: Liz Aneloski
Technical Editor: Diana Roberts
Copy Editor: Judith M. Moretz
Design Director: Diane Pedersen
Cover Design: John Cram and Kathy Lee
Book Design: Bobbi Sloan
Illustrator: Donna Yuen
Photography: Sharon Risedorph
Photo Styling for pages 1 and 2: Adrian Gallardo
    & Renee Isabelle Walker, Stephen Reed Flowers
Author photo: Micael Stefanski

Published by C&T Publishing
P.O. Box 1456
Lafayette, California 94549

ISBN: 1-57120-029-0

ACKNOWLEDGMENTS

Thank you to:

Todd and Tony Hensley for your continued support; Rob Weller, Gary Grossman and Stephanie Kleinman for opening the door of opportunity and pushing me through; Diana Roberts and Liz Aneloski for an excellent eleventh hour effort; Linda Ballou for loving honesty and the ability to keep a secret; Margaret Peters for opening her heart and her home to me for the cover photograph; The New Home Sewing Machine Company, Olfa Products, P&B Textiles, and Omnigrid for excellent products; My family who puts up with my crazy lifestyle; and last but not least, to cousin Jack who makes a killer poppy seed cake.

Introduction.....................4

Tools 6

Rotary Cutter, Rotary Mat, Rotary Ruler, Scissors, Pins, Thread, Seam Ripper, Iron, Sewing Machine

Fabric 8

Grain of the Fabric, Preparing the Fabric

The Basics....................10

Rotary Cutting, Pinning, Stitching, Pressing, Settings, Borders, Decisions, Decisions, Decisions

Projects 15

Rail Fence Quilt   15
Nine Patch Variation Quilt   18
Log Cabin Variation Quilt   22
Friendship Star Quilt   25
Flying Geese Quilt   28
Sampler Quilt (for inspiration)   32

Finishing......................34

Planning the Quilting, Backing, Batting, Layering, Basting, Quilting, Binding

INTRODUCTION

A quilt is like a sandwich. It has three layers:

The quilt top is usually made of many 100 percent cotton fabrics cut in various sizes then sewn together either by hand or machine. *This is called piecing.*

The middle layer is called the batting. It is usually either polyester or 100 percent cotton.

The backing is another piece of 100 percent cotton fabric. Cotton fabric is usually 42" wide, so if the quilt top exceeds 42", it is necessary to sew pieces of fabric together (piece) to create a wide enough piece of fabric for the backing.

All three layers are then stitched together either by hand or machine, uniting all three components as one. *This is called quilting.*

I can remember the first quilt I ever made. My grandma started a Grandmother's Flower Garden quilt in the 1930s and was pleased as punch when I expressed a desire to finish it. What she didn't know was that I was one month and one unit short of graduating from college and had contracted the project to fulfill that requirement. I had not only a fantasy of graduating with a BA in Art, but dreams of snuggling under my hand pieced and quilted queen-size quilt on a cold winter night. Needless to say, I graduated, but with a quilt the size of a bath mat. I had originally planned to be a weaver, but visions of quilts danced in my head. As they say, "The rest is history." I'm a quilter for life.

I love quilts, and have been fortunate enough to be a participant during the past two decades, in the renaissance and evolution of quiltmaking. It has become a sophisticated art form with many different avenues to explore. On Home and Garden Television's® quilt show *Simply Quilts* (of which I am host), we have taped several different episodes, each presenting an expert quilter who shared his/her latest technique or approach to quiltmaking. This craft keeps getting more innovative, and there is always a new method on the horizon. I can remember when rotary cutters were introduced to the quiltmaking world, and now we can generate quilts on computers and even scan images to print our own fabric!

Rail Fence

Log Cabin Variation

Nine Patch

Nine Patch Variation

Friendship Star

Flying Geese

Whether or not this time-honored craft has reached its peak is often discussed. Are there any new quilters out there? The answer is *yes* and it is *you!* I am often asked where a person interested in quilting should begin, so I decided to write this book to get the beginning quilter started with the basics. You must remember that there are many different approaches to quiltmaking, one not better than the others, just different. What this book provides for you is an introduction to the world of rotary cut quiltmaking (as opposed to the templates that my grandma used), using six simple wall quilts you can complete on your own using six basic 6" finished quilt blocks. Fabric requirements are based on 42" wide fabric.

I recommend that you start with a small project as your first quilt. You will be able to finish it and feel successful. I find that when first-time quilters start with a large project, the whole process becomes overwhelming, and they either give up in frustration or lose the enjoyment of the process. Besides, if you start small, you can begin another quilt sooner.

I have chosen six quilt patterns using the three most basic shapes that quilters work with all the time: squares, rectangles, and triangles.

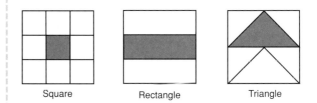

Square   Rectangle   Triangle

If you find that you really enjoy making one of these patterns, you can make more blocks than those required for the wall-size quilt to complete a larger quilt any size you want. The dimensions below are the measurements of the mattress *top* only. To determine the quilt size be sure to include the amount you want to hang down the sides of the mattress in your calculations.

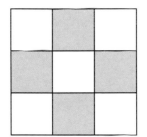

Rail Fence

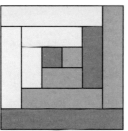

Log Cabin Variation

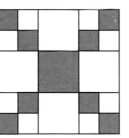

Nine Patch

Nine Patch Variation

Standard Mattress Sizes:

Three Year Crib:	23" x 46"
Six Year Crib:	27" x 52"
Twin:	39" x 75"
Full:	54" x 75"
Queen:	60" x 80"
King:	76" x 80"

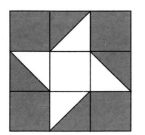

Friendship Star

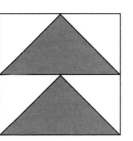

Flying Geese

My hope for you is that through making these projects you will become familiar with the basics of quiltmaking and develop into a quilt lover, as I have. Good luck, and don't blame me if your family never sees the whites of your eyes again—they will get used to it.

TOOLS

Quilters love gadgets, and every year more tools are introduced to the quiltmaking world. Your first visit to a quilt shop or the quilting section of a fabric store can be overwhelming. There are many decisions that need to be made when purchasing the necessary tools to get started quilting. Where do you begin? The following shopping list provides the must-haves for anyone getting started. Many of the products come in different sizes. Please obtain the recommended sizes. You will not be satisfied in the long run if you skimp. Later on you might want to add more or less expensive companion supplies, but the following are the best sizes to start with. The initial investment will seem costly, but these tools will serve you for years if taken care of properly. (See pages 36-37 for the supplies needed for quilting.)

ROTARY CUTTER

This is a rolling razor blade mounted on a plastic handle. This tool is extremely dangerous and should be kept away from children. I recommend the medium-size cutter.

ROTARY MAT

This is a self-healing plastic mat that must be used in conjunction with the rotary cutter. I recommend either the 11" x 17" or 17" x 23" size. The smaller one is great for starting out or taking to a quilting class. The larger one is more versatile. Eventually you will want both.

ROTARY RULER

This is a ruler made especially for use with the rotary cutter and mat. It has ⅛" increments marked in both directions, and is thick enough not to be cut when used with the rotary cutter. You will eventually have many rulers, but to start with I recommend the Omnigrid® 6" x 12".

SCISSORS

A small shear with a sharp tip, four to five inches long. These are used for clipping unwanted threads and fabric tips (bunny ears).

PINS

Extra-long fine glass-head pins. I know these are costly, but the less expensive bargain brands are thick and will cause distortion when lining up seams (I watch for the good ones to go on sale and stock up).

THREAD

You will want to use a quality cotton thread. You can either match it to the project you are working on or purchase a neutral gray or tan.

SEAM RIPPER

I hate to sound negative, but yes, even the seasoned quilter uses one. Splurge and get yourself a quality one (you'll know by the price). Cheap, dull rippers will cause more problems than they are worth by stretching the fabric.

IRON

The one you have in your closet is probably just fine, but eventually you might want to purchase a super hot steam iron. Correct pressing is very important to making a successful quilt.

SEWING MACHINE

Like cars, there are many different makes on the market. Eventually this may be your biggest purchase. But for your first quilt you need one that is in good working condition, with proper tension, an even stitch, and a good, sharp size 80 needle.

That's it! The rest of the tools are gravy. However, if you are like most quilters, one day you will look into your sewing room and realize the amount you paid for the contents could have put your first-born through medical school. But shhh, don't tell anyone.

ROTARY CUTTER

ROTARY MAT

OMNIMAT

Omnigrid

ROTARY RULER

PINS

SCISSORS

THREAD

SEAM RIPPER

FABRIC

Quilting stores are found all over the world and it is here we can get the finest 100 percent cottons available. Different grades of fabric are used for the printed fabrics available to us. You want to use the best you can find. The less expensive cottons are loosely woven with a lesser thread count per inch and will only cause you problems in the end. Stay away from poly/cotton blends. They will shrink right before your eyes as you press the shapes.

As an avid fabric lover and collector, the thought of starting from scratch seems foreign to me. Upon reflection, I realize I was not really confident with fabric choices until I had made several quilts. The fabric will dictate the mood or look of your quilt. Each quilt in this book uses a different approach to fabric selection, which is briefly discussed at the onset of each project. Once you have decided what look you want, there are two vital rules to keep in mind.
1. Always use light, medium-colored, and dark fabrics. Look how example A is composed only of mediums. It lacks the punch that example C has. Medium fabrics are usually the most appealling, but force yourself to integrate both lights and darks. Using a combination of lights, mediums, and darks will make your quilt sparkle.

2. Use printed fabric with variety in the character of the print. This refers to the design and scale of the print on the cloth. Often new quiltmakers come to the sport with an image of what quilting fabrics should look like—small calicos. When you use only one type of print your quilt may look like it has the chicken pox. See how much more interesting example C is than example B? This is because C not only has light, medium, and dark prints, it also contains fabric with different characters of print, or visual texture. There are fabulous prints in delicious colors available to us. Never judge a fabric by how it looks on the bolt. We are not making clothing. Remember, when the fabric is cut up it will look quite different.

Try this trick: Take a 4" square of cardboard and cut a 2" square hole in the center. Position it over the fabric to see how it will "read" when used in patchwork.

Be open to using fabrics that might make you feel uncomfortable. Remember, you aren't wearing the fabric, you are cutting it into little pieces and making a quilt. Experiment. That is how I grew to love and understand fabric relationships.

Examples of blocks using light, medium, and dark fabrics and a variety in the character of the prints.

8

Grain of the Fabric

When fabric is produced the threads are woven in two directions, creating a length and a width. This is called the straight of grain. If you cut diagonally across the grain (in triangle pieces) you are working on the bias. Bias edges must be sewn and pressed carefully, since they stretch easily. The long finished edge of the fabric is called the selvage. Always trim off the selvage edge since it can cause distortion of the block and is difficult to hand quilt through.

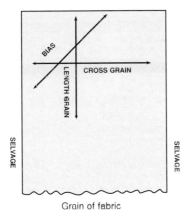

Grain of fabric

Preparing the Fabric

There are different schools of thought as to whether or not you should prewash your fabric.

My philosophy is that you should, and here are my three reasons:

1. When the quilt is laundered, 100 percent cotton can shrink causing puckers and distortion of the shape.

2. Darker color dyes have been known to migrate to the lighter fabrics in quilts. This defines the expression "heartbreak."

3. Fabric is treated with chemicals, and I don't think it is healthy to breathe or handle these chemicals over an extended period of time. I have found myself wheezing when I decided to pass up prewashing.

If you are working with a dark piece of fabric (reds and purples are extremely suspect), test your fabric by cutting a two-inch square and putting it in boiling water. See if any color migrates. If it does, soak your fabric in a half-and-half solution of white vinegar and water. Dry and retest the fabric. If it still runs, repeat the solution process. If the fabric continues to run, toss it. It could ruin your quilt.

> Always prewash darks and lights separately.

THE BASICS

Rotary Cutting

I love rotary cutting. Please practice this technique on some scrap fabric before starting on your project.

When rotary cutting strips of fabric, fold the fabric selvage to selvage and then fold again lining up the straight of the grain as much as possible. This will give you four layers of fabric to cut through.

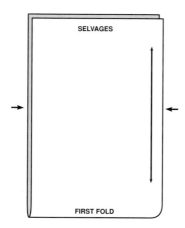

Fold the fabric.

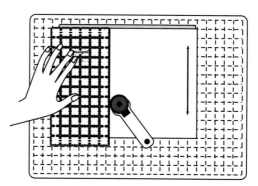

Line up the edge of the fabric with the grid on the cutting mat.

Position the fabric on the mat, keeping all sides of the fabric in line with the grid of the mat. (Avoid letting the fabric hang off the edge of the table.)

The following instructions are for right-handed cutting. For left-handed cutting, turn the illustration upside down.

Line up the vertical marks on the ruler with the grid on the cutting mat. Place the ruler ½" over the raw edges of the fabric. Be careful to position your hand so that none of your fingers are hanging over the side of the ruler where you will be cutting. Rest your pinkie finger on the outside of the ruler. This will not only help protect your finger, but will also keep the ruler from moving.

Position the ruler for rotary cutting.

Place the rotary cutter blade right next to the ruler. Depress the safety latch of the cutter, exposing the blade, and make a single pass (cutting away from your body) through the entire length of the fabric to remove the uneven raw edges.

Move the ruler over 1" (to cut a 1" strip), lining up the vertical 1" mark on the ruler with the edge of the fabric. Line up one of the horizontal lines on the ruler with one of the horizontal grid lines on the mat and the folded edge of the fabric. Cut the 1" strip. Practice this a few times to get the hang of it. Follow this same process to cut the strips needed for your quilting projects.

If the strip of fabric you are cutting is wider than your ruler, use the grid lines on your rotary mat to help you cut this wider strip.

Retract the rotary cutter blade after every cut. Rotary cutters are very sharp. This is a good habit to develop from the start.

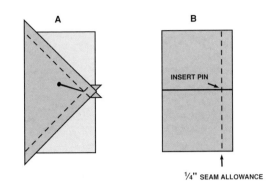

Pin two points of a shape to align exactly.

Pinning

As you become acquainted with different quilters and quilting techniques you will meet those people who pin and those who don't. I have found that the little time it takes to pin can determine the success of the block. Basically, you should pin where there are seams and intersections that need to line up. Here are a few guidelines:

1. When aligning seams that are pressed in opposite directions, place a pin in both sides of the seam no more than ⅛" from each side.

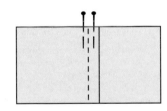

Pinning seams pressed in opposite directions

2. If you have two points of a shape that need to align exactly, place the first pin in the wrong side of A (exactly at the intersection), inserting it into the right side of B (exactly into the ¼" seam allowance). Press the head of the pin firmly into both intersections.

While holding the first pin tautly in place, place the second and third pin on each side of the intersection, no more than ⅛" from the first pin. Let the first pin dangle loosely. As you stitch and approach the intersection, remove the first pin at the last second and let the sewing machine needle drop into that hole. If your sewing machine doesn't sew over pins easily, remove the second and third pins right before you stitch over them. I have found this is a great technique, and encourage you to develop this habit.

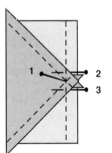

Remove pin from the intersection at the last second.

Stitching

Set the stitch length on your machine just long enough so that your seam ripper slides nicely in under the stitch. Backtacking is not necessary for the projects in this book, because all the seam ends will be enclosed by other seams.

¼-Inch Seam Allowance

To piece the quilt top, you always use a ¼" seam allowance. The shapes in this book are all cut with the seam allowance included. Put your clear plastic rotary ruler under the sewing machine needle and drop the presser foot, then ease the needle down on top of the ¼" mark. Take a thin piece of masking tape and mark the ¼" on the throat plate, using the edge of the ruler as your guide. Many machines have an exact ¼" foot. If yours does, you are home free.

As you sew the fabric pieces together with the right sides together and the raw edges aligned, use the piece of tape as your guide. This is an extremely important step to ensure accuracy. Take the time to understand your machine's ¼ inch. My kids' term, "Close enough," will only reward you with yards of frustration.

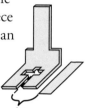

Mark the ¼" seam allowance.

To check your ¼ inch, Sally Collins of Walnut Creek, California, recommends that you cut two strips of fabric 1" x 3½". Sew the two strips together, press, and measure. The sewn unit should be 1½" wide. If not, try again until you find your machine's perfect ¼ inch.

Seam Ripping

On occasion you will want to pick out a seam. Cut every third stitch on one side of the fabric, then lift the thread off the other side of the fabric.

If you have two bias edges sewn together, as in the Flying Geese block on page 28 , consider throwing the unit away and starting over. The chance of stretching the bias pieces is almost 100 percent. If the pieces stretch, they won't line up and fit properly when they are stitched to the next section.

Pressing

This is a very important area of quiltmaking. Many beginners approach the pressing portion of quiltmaking as if they were ironing the weekly laundry. Old habits are hard to break, but you must learn this technique if you want to have super looking quilts.

1. Press on a firm surface (an ironing board with a single pad). Usually seams are pressed in one direction or the other (not open). Press the way the arrows indicate in my instructions. This helps with seam alignment in your block construction.

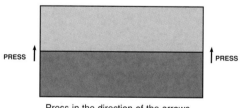

Press in the direction of the arrows.

2. When moving seams in one direction or the other, press the pieced units from the right side of the fabric. This will avoid pressing tucks into the sewn seams.

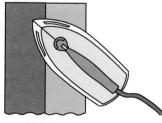

Pressing

Settings

All the projects in this book are placed in a straight set to form the quilt top. A straight set is the easiest, therefore the best, way to begin. The blocks are positioned with the sides vertical and horizontal to the quilt's edges, not diagonal ("on point" in quilter's language). First arrange the blocks in a pleasing manner, then sew the blocks into rows and press. Once the rows are sewn and pressed, sew each row to the next row. Press as the arrows indicate.

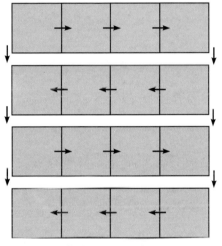

Straight set, pressing

Borders

Measure your sewn quilt top across the center of the quilt from top to bottom and from one side to the other side. Compare your measurements to the measurements in the instructions. If your ¼" seam allowance is off, this is where the difference will show up.

Cut the top and bottom border strips the length measured (above), by the width given in the quilt instructions. Find the center of the quilt top and the center of the top border strip by folding them in half. Pin them together with the right sides together matching the centers. Pin the ends of the border strip to the corners of the quilt top and every 2" in between. Sew and press, following the pressing arrows. Repeat for the bottom border.

Measure your quilt top from top to bottom across the center including the borders. Cut the side border strips this length by the width given in the quilt instructions. Pin and sew as above to attach the side borders.

Inner border

Repeat for the outer border.

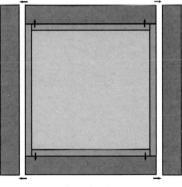

Outer border

Note: If your quilt is longer vertically than it is horizontally, you might want to cut and attach the side borders first, then the top and bottom, to save fabric, as in the Friendship Star quilt (page 25).

Decisions, Decisions, Decisions

Keeping the previous tips in mind, choose either the Rail Fence, Log Cabin Variation, or Nine Patch Variation block to get started.

Rail Fence

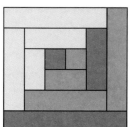

Log Cabin Variation

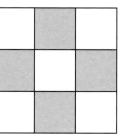

Nine Patch

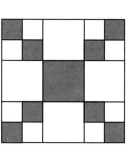

Nine Patch Variation

These patterns are made of shapes that are on the grain of the fabric and will not stretch or distort when you are working with them.

After you have completed one or all of these projects, try your hand at the Friendship Star or Flying Geese blocks.

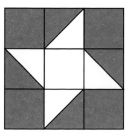

Friendship Star

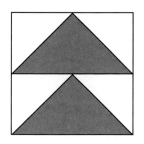

Flying Geese

These blocks are a little harder to make because they have triangular shapes. Whenever you work with triangles there is a risk of stretching the cloth as a result of bias edges. If you make a mistake or two, don't fret. This is a learning process. Enjoy it.

After you have pieced the top, you will have to decide if you want to hand or machine quilt your project. I prefer hand quilting, since it lends a softer, homespun look. However, hand quilting does require a significant amount of time, and if this is a quilt that kids are going to drag around or made for a bed that the dogs jump on (I know about these things), I would definitely machine quilt. Your decision rests entirely on the look you want to achieve and/or the destination of the quilt. Make this decision after your top is complete. (Please refer to the Finishing chapter on page 34).

Quiltmaking is a journey both men and women have loved for generations. We all started at the same place so there's no need to feel intimidated by a lack of experience. That only means you have more opportunities to develop your skills. Welcome to the wonderful world, and people, of quiltmaking!

RAIL FENCE QUILT

This wallhanging is $40\frac{1}{2}$" x $40\frac{1}{2}$" and is made up of twenty-five 6" Rail Fence blocks.

RAIL FENCE QUILT

Fabric Tips:

Pastel quilts are not normally my personal choice. However, when I visited my local quilt store, the beautiful floral fabric in the border, containing these light, delicate colors, had just arrived. I had found my focus fabric. Perfect for my rail fence! I decided to work with the two most predominant colors in this border print, which directed me to the pink and green sections of the shop. I chose three pink fabrics (pink color family) and three green fabrics (green color family), each with an unusual size and scale of print, and then I went to the beige section and chose another three fabrics. That's not really many decisions; you can do it!

> Focus Fabric—
> Let the colors in your main print dictate the look of the quilt.

Fabric Requirements

Focus fabric for outer border:
   ¾ yard
Green:
   ¼ yard each of three different fabrics
Pink:
   ¼ yard each of three different fabrics
Beige:
   ¼ yard each of three different fabrics
Stripe for inner border:
   ¼ yard
Binding:
   ¼ yard
Backing:
   1¼ yards

Please read <u>The Basics</u> chapter before starting.

Cutting

Rail Fence

Cut two 2½" x 42" strips from each of the nine fabrics (page 10).

Piecing and Pressing

1. Sew one of each of the three different green strips together (page 12). This set should measure 6½" wide. Make two sets. Press as the arrows indicate.

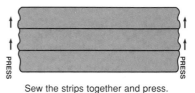

Sew the strips together and press.

2. Repeat for the pink and beige fabrics. You will now have two sewn 6½" strips of each color family.

3. Trim the left end straight (page 10).

4. Cut the sewn set into 6½" blocks (same technique as for cutting strips). You will need 8 green, 8 pink, and 9 beige blocks.

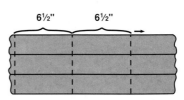

Cut the units.

> This process is called strip piecing.

5. Lay out your blocks as shown. Note that they are in a straight set (page 13).

6. Sew the blocks into rows and then sew the rows together (page 13). Refer to page 12 for pressing.
   Your top should measure 30½" x 30½". If it does, use the instructions below to cut and attach the inner and outer border strips. If it doesn't, see page 13 to measure and cut the correct border lengths for your quilt top.

Inner border:

7. Cut two strips 1½" x 30½" for the top and bottom and two strips 1½" x 32½" for the sides.

8. Sew on the inner border (first the shorter top and bottom strips, then the longer side strips). Press.

Outer border:

9. Cut two strips 5½" x 32½" for the top and bottom and two strips 5½" x 42½" for the sides.

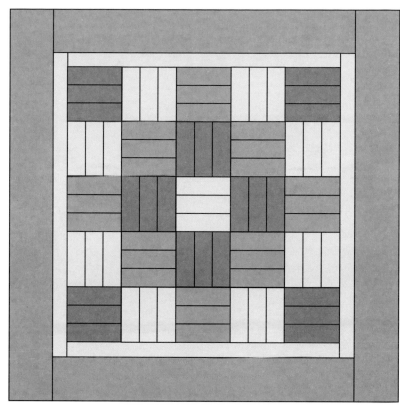

Rail Fence Quilt

10. Sew on the outer border (first the shorter top and bottom strips, then the longer side strips). Press.

Yeah! I knew you could do it. Now it's time to decide how to handle the quilting and finishing details. Please refer to the Finishing chapter beginning on page 34.

NINE PATCH
VARIATION QUILT

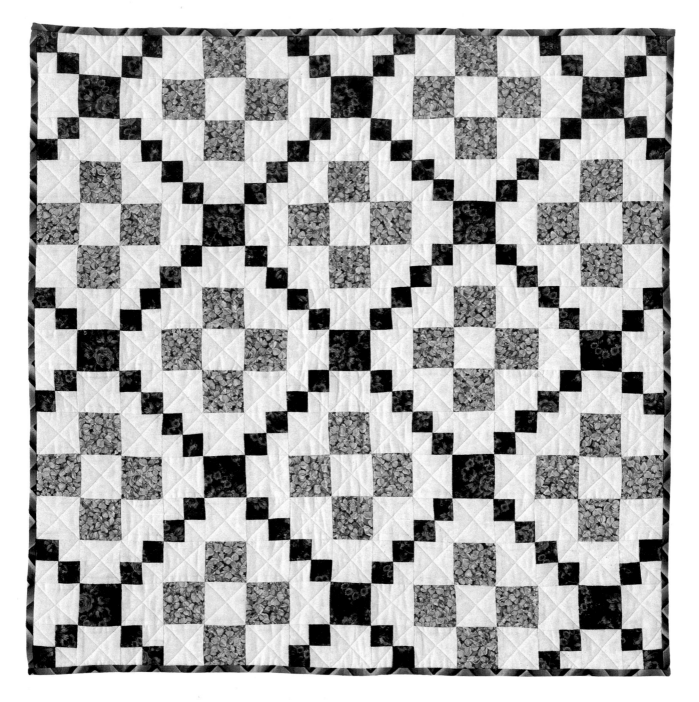

This wallhanging is 30½" x 30½" and is made up of twelve 6" Nine Patch blocks
and thirteen 6" Nine Patch Variation blocks.

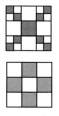

NINE PATCH VARIATION QUILT

Fabric Tips

Everyone loves blue and white quilts. They are always crisp and clean looking. The beauty of this charming little quilt is that you only need to pick two blues (blue color family) and one white fabric. Stunning results are insured with this monochromatic color scheme.

> Monochromatic—
> Working with only
> one color family.

Fabric Requirements

Dark blue:
  ½ yard
Medium blue:
  ⅓ yard
White:
  1 yard
Binding:
  ¼ yard
Backing:
  1 yard

Please read <u>The Basics</u> chapter before starting.

Nine Patch Blocks

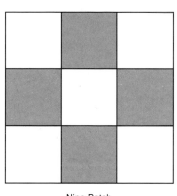

Nine Patch

Cutting

Medium blue:
  Cut four 2½" x 42" strips (page 10).
White:
  Cut five 2½" x 42" strips.

Piecing and Pressing

Press as the arrows indicate (page 12).

1. Set A: Sew a white strip to each long edge of a medium blue strip. Repeat to make a second Set A. Press.

2. Cut Sets A into twenty-four 2½" segments (same technique as for cutting strips).

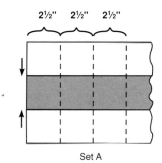

Set A

3. Set B: Sew a medium blue strip to each long edge of a white strip. Press.

4. Cut Set B into twelve 2½" segments.

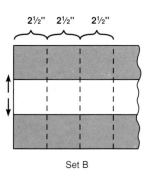

Set B

5. Arrange and sew Sets A and B as shown into twelve Nine Patch blocks, matching the seams and pinning (page 11). Press.

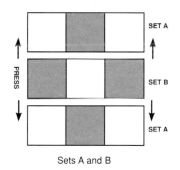

Sets A and B

Nine Patch Variation Blocks

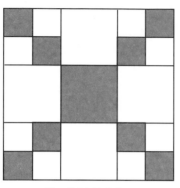

Nine Patch Variation

Cutting

Dark Blue:
Cut four 1½" x 42" strips and one 2½" x 42" strip.
White:
Cut four 1½" x 42" strips and four 2½" x 42" strips.

Piecing and Pressing

6. Set C: Sew four pairs of the dark blue and white 1½" strips together. Press.

7. Cut Sets C into one hundred and four 1½" segments.

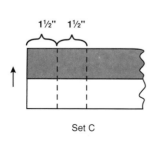

Set C

8. Sew Sets C together in pairs as shown (Four Patch block). Press.

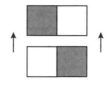

Four Patch

9. Cut twenty-six white 2½" squares from two of the strips.

10. Arrange the Four Patch blocks and white squares and sew as shown. Press.

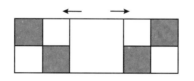

Set C Unit

11. Set D: Sew two white and one dark blue 2½" strips as shown. Press. Cut into 2½" segments.

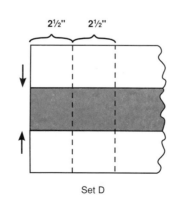

Set D

Set D

12. Arrange and sew Set C Units and Sets D together as shown into thirteen Nine Patch Variation blocks, matching the seams and pinning. Press.

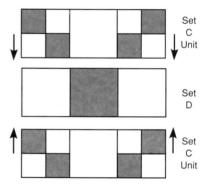

Set C Unit

Set D

Set C Unit

Arrange, sew, and press.

This is called strip piecing and using a block combination.

13. Lay out your Nine Patch and Nine Patch Variation blocks as shown. Note that they are in a straight set.

14. Sew the blocks into rows, press, and then sew the rows together (page 13). Press. Refer to page 12 for pressing.

Great job! I hope you love your Nine Patch Variation quilt as much as I love mine. Please turn to page 34 for additional information to help you finish up your little treasure.

Nine Patch Variation Quilt

LOG CABIN
VARIATION QUILT

This quilt measures 36½" x 36½" and is made up of sixteen 6" Log Cabin Variation blocks.

LOG CABIN VARIATION QUILT

Fabric and Design Tips

Log Cabin quilts are great. Not only are they graphically pleasing and filled with symbolism, but they are easy! Usually the center square is red. It is called the chimney, representing the hearth of the home. The outer rectangles surrounding the chimney are referred to as the logs.

There are several variations of the Log Cabin block. Typically one half of the logs are light and the other half are dark. The block we are working with is actually an off-center Log Cabin since there is not an equal number of light and dark logs. The log strips are chosen randomly to get the scrap look. As for my fabric choice, season by season Mother Nature brings us a different color palette. I love the fall with its crisp air and delicious hues of red, orange, and brown. When I saw this outer border fabric I knew it was perfect for my Log Cabin quilt.

> Look to Mother Nature for color inspirations.

Fabric Requirements

Seasonal fabric for outer border and logs:
   1¼ yards
Red chimney and binding:
   ⅓ yard
Darks:
   ¼ yard each of five different fabrics (I used the border fabric for the sixth log)
Lights:
   ¼ yard each of four different fabrics
Inner border:
   ¼ yard
Backing:
   1¼ yards

Please read The Basics chapter before starting.

Cutting

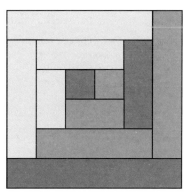

Log Cabin Variation

Chimney:
   Cut sixteen 1½" x 1½" squares.
Dark logs:
   Cut three strips 1½" x 42" of each dark fabric.

Light logs:
   Cut three strips 1½" x 42" of each light fabric.

LOG CABIN VARIATION BLOCK CONSTRUCTION

The following instructions are for one Log Cabin block.

1. Sew a dark strip onto a red chimney square. Press as the arrows indicate (away from the center of the block). Using your rotary cutter and ruler, trim the strip even with the edges of the red square as shown (Unit A).

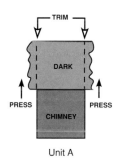

Unit A

2. Sew a dark strip onto Unit A. Press and trim (Unit B).

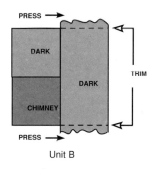

Unit B

3. Rotate the block so the previously sewn log is at the top. Sew a light strip onto Unit B. Press and trim (Unit C).

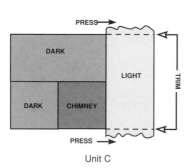

Unit C

4. Rotate the blocks as in Step 3. Sew a light strip onto unit C. Press and trim (Unit D).

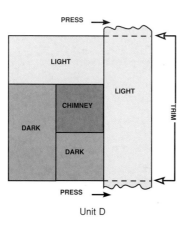

Unit D

The key to a Log Cabin block is to keep working your way around the block clockwise with this pattern in mind: Chimney, dark, dark, light, light, dark, dark, light, light, dark, dark. Sew 16 blocks.

> Always keep the previously sewn log at the top.

5. Lay out your blocks as shown or choose your own layout. Note that they are in a straight set (page 13.)

6. Sew the blocks into rows, press, and then sew the rows together (page 13). Refer to page 12 for pressing.

Your quilt top should measure 24½" x 24½". If it does, use the instructions below to cut and attach the inner and outer border strips. If it doesn't, see page 13 to measure and cut the correct border lengths for your quilt top.

Inner border:

7. Cut two strips 1½" x 24½" for the top and bottom and two strips 1½" x 26½" for the sides.

8. Sew on the inner border (first the shorter top and bottom strips, then the longer side strips). Press. Refer to page 12 for pressing.

Outer border:

9. Cut two strips 5½" x 26½" for the top and bottom and two strips 5½" x 36½" for the sides.

10. Sew on the outer border (first the shorter top and bottom strips, then the longer side strips). Press.

Because of the strong diagonal movement of color, you can get many different looks by rotating the blocks. Once all your blocks are complete, feel free to play with the arrangement before you sew them together. You might like your set better than the one I decided on. Please refer to the Finishing chapter beginning on page 34 to finish your wonderful Log Cabin quilt.

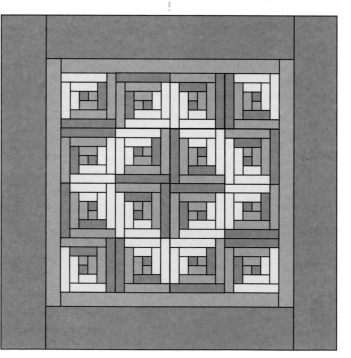

Log Cabin Variation Quilt

FRIENDSHIP STAR QUILT

This quilt measures 34$\frac{1}{2}$" x 36$\frac{1}{2}$" and is made up of sixteen 6" Friendship Star blocks.

FRIENDSHIP STAR QUILT

Now it's time to tackle triangles! The Friendship Star is basically a Nine Patch block with half-square triangles at the top, bottom, and on each side. Half-square triangles are easy to work with. My only caution is that you have now entered the world of exposed cut bias edges. Here are two rules to keep in mind when working with triangles:

1. Never press the fabric triangle after it has been cut and before it has been sewn. You stand a big chance of stretching the exposed cut bias edge.

2. Never pull the units through the sewing machine as you stitch them together, since this can stretch the shape. Let your machine do the work for you, not your hands.

Fabric Tips

My daughter Adair loves purple and teal! These particular colors are not necessarily my first choice, but they certainly are hers. I looked at her bedding set and worked with the colors that were reflected in it. There are different color relationships in our everyday environment, from Mother Nature to the window display at your favorite clothing store. Become aware of your surroundings and learn from them. This is how you become comfortable with unexplored color relationships.

Fabric Requirements

Focus fabric for outer border and binding:
  1 yard
Light for stars:
  ¼ yard each of two different fabrics
Dark for block backgrounds:
  ¼ yard each of nine different fabrics
Checked fabric for sashing:
  ¼ yard
Inner border:
  ¼ yard
Backing:
  1 yard

Please read The Basics chapter before starting.

Cutting

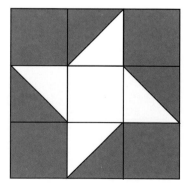
Friendship Star

The following numbers are for one Friendship Star. You will need sixteen in all.

Star:
  Cut one 2½" square for the star center.
  Cut two 2⅞" squares, then cut in half diagonally from corner to corner for the star points.

Background:
  Cut four 2½" squares for the block corners.
  Cut two 2⅞" squares, then cut in half diagonally for the block background.

Cutting half-square triangles

Piecing and Pressing

1. Sew one star triangle to one background triangle along the long side. Press.

2. Repeat three times.

Star points

3. Lay out and sew the block as shown. Press as the arrows indicate. Sew 16 blocks.

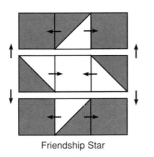

Friendship Star

4. Lay out your blocks as shown. Note that they are in a straight set (page 13).

5. Sew together each row of four stars, being sure to match the seams and pin. Page 11. Press.

Checked sashing:

6. Your rows should measure 24½". If they do, cut two strips 1½" x 24½". If they don't, cut the sashing strips the measurement of your rows.

7. Insert the two rows of sashing and sew the rows together. Press.

Your quilt top should measure 24½" x 26½". If it does, use the following instructions to cut and attach the inner and outer border strips. If it doesn't, see page 13 to measure and cut the correct border lengths for your quilt top.

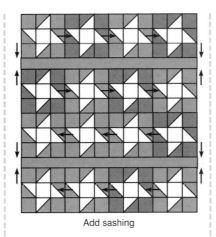

Add sashing

Inner border:

This quilt is a rectangle, so to conserve fabric, the side borders are sewn on first, before the top and bottom borders.

8. Cut four strips 1½" x 26½".

9. Sew on the inner border (first the side strips, then the top and bottom).

Outer border:

10. Sew on the outer border (first the side shorter strips, then the top and bottom).

You did it! Welcome to the wonderful world of stars. They are my all-time favorites. Now it's time to quilt and finish your Friendship Star Quilt (see Finishing chapter beginning on page 34). I hope you learn to love stars as I do.

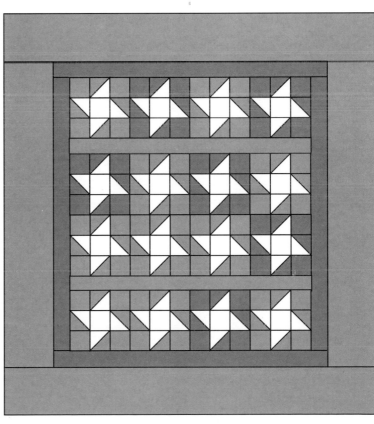

Friendship Star Quilt

FLYING GEESE QUILT

This quilt measures 34" x 34" and contains thirty-two Flying Geese blocks.

FLYING GEESE QUILT

Flying Geese are made using quarter-square triangles and half-square triangles. Although the triangles both have 45, 45, and 90 degree angle corners, they are very different. The half-square triangle has two edges that are on the straight of grain. The quarter-square triangle has only one edge that is on the straight of grain.

This is very important because when sewn, you always want the outside edge of the block on the straight of grain. This avoids unnecessary stretching.

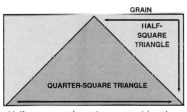

Half-square and quarter-square triangles

CUTTING A HALF-SQUARE TRIANGLE:

First cut a square at the given measurement, then cut the square exactly corner to corner. This will give you two half-square triangles.

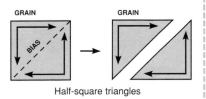

Half-square triangles

CUTTING A QUARTER-SQUARE TRIANGLE:

First cut a square at the given measurement, then cut the square exactly corner to corner, two times. This will give you four quarter-square triangles.

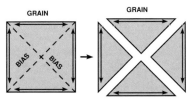

Quarter-square triangles

The difference between a half-square and a quarter-square triangle is the location of the bias edge.

Remember when working with triangles:

1. Never press the fabric shape after it has been cut and before it has been sewn. You stand a big chance of stretching the exposed cut bias edge.

2. Never pull the units through the sewing machine as you stitch them together, since this can stretch the shapes. Let your machine do the work for you, not your hands.

Fabric Tips

I love the Fourth of July. As a family, we have always celebrated America's birthday with much fervor and gusto. My natural inclination is to always work with red, white, and blue! Holidays provide a simple solution for choosing fabric. This approach always works, with guaranteed results.

> Simply think of your favorite holiday and work with the colors associated with it.

Fabric Requirements

Holiday fabric for outer border:
   1 yard
Red:
   ¼ yard each of two different fabrics
Blue:
   ¼ yard each of two different fabrics
Background:
   ½ yard
Inner border:
   ¼ yard
Binding:
   ¼ yard
Backing:
   1 yard

Please read The Basics chapter before starting.

Cutting

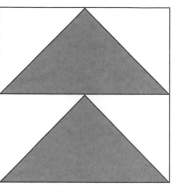

Flying Geese

Red:
Cut four squares 7¼" x 7¼", then cut in half diagonally twice. Yields 16 quarter-square triangles.

Blue:
Cut four squares 7¼" x 7¼", then cut in half diagonally twice. Yields 16 quarter-square triangles.

Light background:
Cut thirty-two squares 3⅞" x 3⅞", then cut in half diagonally. Yields 64 half-square triangles.

Piecing and Pressing

1. Piece one half-square triangle to one quarter-square triangle, lining up the outer corners as shown. Press as the arrows indicate.

2. Repeat for the other side. Press.

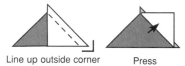

Line up outside corner   Press

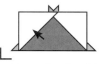

Repeat for other side

3. Trim off the bunny ears.

Trim bunny ears

4. Lay out eight Flying Geese blocks as shown.

5. Sew the Flying Geese blocks together to form one large block. Piece and press as the arrows indicate. Repeat to form four large blocks.

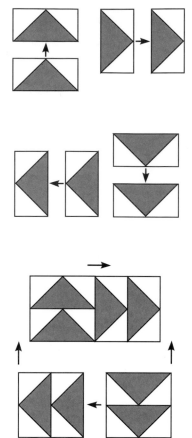

Sew the blocks together.

6. Sew the blocks into rows and then sew the rows together (page 13.). Press.

Your quilt should measure 24½" x 24½". If it does, use the following instructions to cut and attach the inner and outer border strips. If it doesn't, see page 13 to measure and cut the correct border lengths for your quilt top.

Inner border:

7. Cut two strips 1½" x 24½" for the top and bottom and two strips 1½" x 26½" for the sides.

8. Sew on the top and bottom inner border, then the sides. Press.

Outer border:

9. Cut two strips 4½" x 26½" for the top and bottom and two strips 4½" x 34½" for the sides.

10. Sew on the top and bottom outer border, then the sides. Press.

Now it's time to consider the backing, quilting, and binding! See the Finishing chapter beginning on page 34. I know you will enjoy your quilt every year when you take it out to help decorate for your favorite time of year. Happy holidays!

Flying Geese Quilt

SAMPLER QUILT

This quilt measures 40$\frac{1}{2}$" x 40$\frac{1}{2}$" and contains twenty-five 6" blocks.

SAMPLER QUILT

Samplers are a wonderful way to expose yourself to many different techniques without committing to an entire project. As each little quilt was created for this book, I found myself getting carried away with the different patterns. Before I knew it, there was a stack of blocks in the corner of my sewing room that cried, "Don't leave me behind!" It was time to make a sampler. I was amazed at how well the blocks worked together. The magic key was finding a fabric that included all the different colors represented in each quilt block. Right there in my fabric stash was this delightful chicken fabric, perfect! This fabric tied all the colors together and provided a title for this quilt, *Don't Be Chicken.*

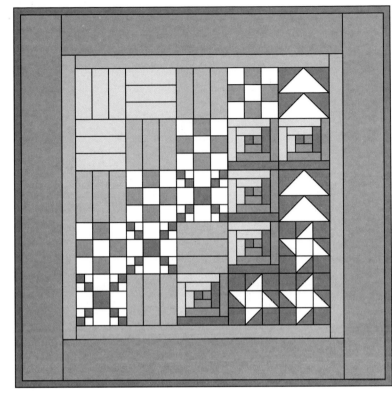

Sampler Quilt

FINISHING

Planning the Quilting

Quilting is the act of stitching all three layers together. Now it's time to consider how you are going to quilt the top—machine or hand. I would suggest you take the time to try hand quilting. I have always enjoyed this part of the process and find that hand quilted quilts have a special look. However, if this is a quilt that the dog is going to nap on, try your hand at machine quilting, since hand quilting is a significant time investment.

Quilting Design

For your first project I recommend that you keep the quilting as simple as possible. You might want to start by quilting "in the ditch." This is done by quilting as close as possible to the seam on the side without a seam allowance. It is a great way for a beginner to start. Your stitches will be hidden, giving you time to perfect the stitch. I also love using simple grids which cover the entire surface. If you look carefully at the projects in this book you will see that I also used some basic quilting designs from clear plastic templates (available at your local quilt store, quilt show, or from a quilt magazine) to add interest. Later in your quilting career you might want to take a class that teaches you how to create your own quilting designs. But for now, in the ditch, basic grid, or simple template will do the job.

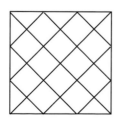

Quilting a grid.

MARKING TOOLS: I usually use a silver Veri-thin™ pencil or white powder chalk. The pencil stays on longer and the chalk comes off easily. Never use a #2 pencil, it may not come out.

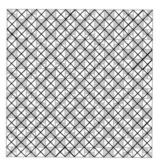

Always test the marking tool to make sure the marks come out, before marking the entire top.

Narrow masking tape is a good way to mark straight lines. Place the tape where desired and make your quilting stitches right next to (not through) the tape.

Creating a Basic Grid

All of the tops in this book are based on 6" blocks. Mark at 2" increments around the edge of the pieced blocks and use your ruler to lightly draw diagonal lines with your marking tool.

Quilting grid marked on Nine Patch Variation

If you decide to incorporate the use of a template as seen in the Rail Fence border, place the template on the quilt top and trace the template design.

Backing

All the projects in this book are 42" wide or less. This eliminates the problem of piecing the backing together. If you get carried away making blocks and find that your quilt is wider than 42", you will have to sew sections of the backing fabric together to create a wide enough piece of fabric. Remember, it's OK to use different cotton prints for one backing. This can be as much fun as deciding the fabric for the front of the quilt. Here are a few things to keep in mind:

1. Always cut off the selvage edges before piecing the fabric together, since it is difficult to hand quilt through the selvages and the seams won't lay flat.

2. If your quilt top has a lot of white in it, as in the Nine Patch on page 18, use light colors for the backing so it doesn't show through the batting to the front.

3. Always prewash and make the backing a few inches larger than the top on all four sides. This is in case your quilt top shifts during quilting.

Never use a sheet or piece of decorator fabric for the backing. They have a high thread count and are difficult to hand quilt.

Batting

For hand quilting I recommend starting with a low-loft polyester batting. It makes the quilting stitch much easier to learn.

For machine quilting I recommend that you use a 100 percent cotton batt. Make sure you follow the instructions if it needs to be prewashed.

Layering

Depending on the size of my project, I either work on a table top, (small quilt) or on my non-loop carpet (large quilt). First you must either tape down (table top), or pin using T pins (carpet), the backing of the quilt *wrong* side up, working from the center of each side to the corners. Keep the fabric grain straight and get the backing stretched taut. No bubbles or ripples are acceptable, or you will have folds and tucks in the back of your finished quilt.

Tape the backing.

Carefully unroll the batting and smooth it on top of the backing. Trim the batting to the same size as the backing. Smooth the quilt top onto the batting right side up.

Basting

For Hand Quilting

Knot one end of the thread and take large stitches through all three layers. Keep the layers straight and square.

> Never baste with a colored thread, since the dye might migrate on to the fabric.

Don't bother knotting the other end of the thread. When it's time to remove the basting you can just give the unknotted end of the thread a little tug and it will pull out.

I like to baste in a grid pattern (about every 4"), so there is an even amount of basting throughout the quilt. Never skimp on this part of the process. It will only cause disaster down the road, since your quilt layers may slip and move during the quilting process.

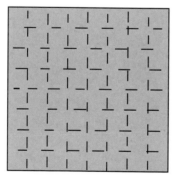

Baste in a grid.

For Machine Quilting

Unlike hand quilting, you will pin baste every 3" with safety pins. Pin evenly across the quilt, staying away from where the quilting stitches will be sewn.

Quilting

Hand Quilting

For hand quilting you will need:

HOOP/FRAME: The number one question asked by beginning quilters about to embark on hand quilting is: Do I really need a frame that sits on the floor? The answer is yes/no! A frame provides excellent tension control and keeps your quilt flat and square. However, it is a substantial investment, and first you must find out if you enjoy hand quilting or not. You will know when it's time to invest in a quilting frame. At that time, shop at the quilt shows and shops, and make sure it has the following three components: Excellent tension control, stability, and easy to assemble. Therefore I recommend starting with a 16" round quilting hoop. Never use an embroidery hoop; they aren't strong enough.

THIMBLE: Forget grandma's thimble from her treasured sewing box. Get a thimble that is made especially for hand quilting. Quilting thimbles have deep indentations that hold the needle.

THREAD: There are several brands on the market, but you want to make sure that it is made especially for hand quilting. It will be marked as quilting thread on the end of the spool. It is a little heavier than regular sewing thread.

NEEDLES: Quilting needles are called "betweens." Start with a #9, and as you learn the stitch, try a higher number. The higher the number, the smaller the needle. I use a #11.

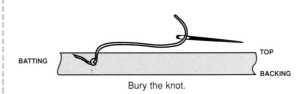

HAND QUILTING STITCHES

Hand quilting is done with a simple running stitch.

A beginner should be thrilled with three stitches to an inch while the seasoned quilter can boast of up to fourteen. The idea is to get comfortable with the motion and try for even stitches. Your stitches will get smaller with practice. Some people take to this like a duck to water. As for myself, my first stitches were two to the inch —and I was darn proud of it! Not to brag, but with practice, I can now boast of being the fastest quilter west of the Mississippi with twelve stitches to the inch. Practice makes perfect!

To get started:

1. Position the basted quilt in your hoop with the quilt top facing up. Always work from the center of the quilt to the outside edge to avoid bubbles. Make sure that the back is as taut as the top; then loosen all three layers just a little (by pushing inside the hoop with your hand), so the needle can be easily manipulated.

2. Put a small single knot in the thread. Insert the needle through the quilt top and batting (not into the backing) an inch away from where you want to start quilting and bring it up where you will start quilting. Gently pull on the thread, running your thumb nail over the knot to help pop the knot inside the layers. This is called "burying" the knot.

BATTING TOP BACKING

Bury the knot.

3. A thimble is a must, and while you might be uncomfortable working with one at first, it will become your most valuable tool. Typically, the thimble is worn on the middle finger. The thimble indentations hold the blunt end of the needle, while your thumb on top and your hand underneath work together to create hills and valleys that the needle will then pass through. This is called the rocking stitch.

4. When you come to the end of your thread, create another single knot and bury it between the three layers. Pull the remaining amount of thread up and carefully snip off the end.

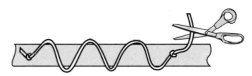

Bury the knot and cut the thread.

Machine Quilting

Machine quilting is an art form of its own. With practice, machine quilting can be a beautiful addition to your quilts.

For machine quilting you will need:

WALKING FOOT: When you sew using a sewing machine, the layers of fabric and batting will not feed in evenly, causing puckers on the backside of the quilt. A walking foot helps to solve this problem.

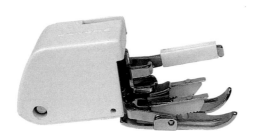

THREAD: Use a fine nylon monofilament thread for the top of the machine and a cotton thread in the bobbin. Use smoke gray if the quilt top is dark, or clear if the quilt top is light.

SAFETY PINS: Unlike hand quilting, you will baste every three inches with safety pins. There are safety pins made especially for machine quilting. They are small and all the same size to keep down the weight of your project.

To start machine quilting, stitch in the ditch or in a grid. (See page 34.) At the beginning and end of each row, backtack with a few stitches. Stitch one row in each direction (closest to the center), both vertically and horizontally, to secure the three layers. Then work from the center out, and quilt the remaining lines. After the center quilting is complete, stitch in the ditch around the border seams and add quilting in the border if desired. Look for templates that are designed for machine quilting.

Your quilt should be supported on all sides. Quilt on a large table. You can use an ironing board adjusted to your table height on your left-hand side, perpendicular to the table.

Ideally your sewing machine should be recessed into your table to create a level surface.

Binding

Trim the batting and backing even with the edges of the quilt top. The binding holds all three layers together, and often gets the most abuse when a quilt is loved and used. There are several ways to approach bindings. I will share the simplest way with you, although later on you might want to experiment with other techniques.

1. Cut two 2¼" x 42" strips. Trim them to the width of the quilt from side to side, plus 1" for trimming. If your quilt is over 42" wide, you will need to piece strips together to get the desired length. Create this union with a seam that is on an angle as shown. This will avoid a big lump in the binding.

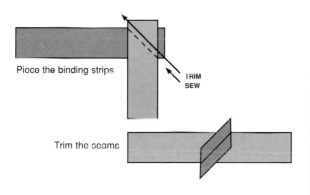

Piece the binding strips

TRIM
SEW

Trim the seams

2. Fold and press lengthwise.

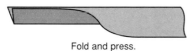

Fold and press.

3. On the top edge of the quilt, line up the raw edges of the binding to the raw edge of the quilt. Let the binding extend ½" past the corners of the quilt. Sew using a ¼" seam allowance. Do this on the top and bottom edges of the quilt.

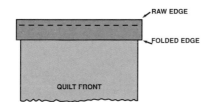

RAW EDGE

FOLDED EDGE

QUILT FRONT

Attach the binding to the front of the quilt.

4. Flip the finished edge of the binding over the raw edge of the quilt and slip stitch the binding to the back side of the quilt. Trim the ends even with the edge of the quilt as shown.

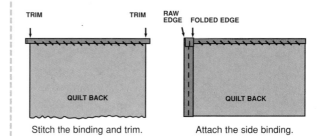

TRIM   TRIM   RAW EDGE   FOLDED EDGE

QUILT BACK   QUILT BACK

Stitch the binding and trim.   Attach the side binding.

5. Cut two 2¼" x 42" strips. For the two remaining sides of the quilt, measure the length of the quilt from top to bottom. Trim the strips to this measurement plus ½" for turning under. Sew the binding strips on, fold over the end of the binding to create a finished edge *before* folding the binding to the back side. Slip stitch down.

You did it! Your first *magnum opus* has been completed. As you travel into the world of quilting, please always keep this in mind—there is not one definitive way to make a quilt. Each teacher has his or her own techniques and personal set of rules. Expose yourself to as many different approaches as possible. Take classes. Check out the local quilting guild. You will meet great people there. Soon you will become comfortable with what works for you. And remember, always sign, date, and document your project on the back side with a permanent marking pen.

Years from now, when you are receiving the blue ribbon for your masterpiece, you will be glad to have commemorated the exact day you were captivated by the satisfying and exciting world of quilting. Until we meet, and we quilters do get around, happy quilting!

ABOUT THE AUTHOR

Alex Anderson's love affair with quiltmaking began in 1978, when she completed her Grandmother's Flower Garden quilt as part of her work toward a degree in art at San Francisco State University. Her study of graphic design in fiber inspired in her a deep respect and admiration for Amish quilts. With their strong visual impact and sensitive intricacy of quilting design, they became the springboard for Alex's quiltmaking. Over the years her central focus has rested upon understanding fabric relationships, and an intense appreciation of traditional quilting surface design and star quilts.

For almost two decades Alex's quilts have been displayed in one-woman shows and have won prizes in group shows. She has lectured to numerous guilds, taught frequently at leading conferences, offered classes at several quilt shops, and currently hosts Home and Garden Television's quilt show *Simply Quilts.* Alex's works have been seen widely in a number of books by Diana McClun, Laura Nownes, Margaret Peters, Mary Coyne Penders, and Charlotte Warr Andersen. Her quilts have been shown in magazines, including several articles specifically about her works. She also worked with her father to develop his company, Sladky Quilt Frames. Her first book, *Quilts for Fabric Lovers*, which celebrates creative use of fabric, was published by C&T Publishing in the fall of 1994 and her second book *Simply Stars*, also published by C&T Publishing, was released in the fall of 1996.

Alex lives in Livermore, California, with her husband, two children, two cats, one dog, pet squirrel, one fish, and the challenges of step-aerobics and suburban life.

The Cotton Patch Mail Order
3405 Hall Lane, Dept. CTB
Lafayette, CA 94549
e-mail: cottonpa@aol.com
800-835-4418 • 510-283-7883
A Complete Quilting Supply Store

If you want to learn more about quilting, try these other books from C&T Publishing:

An Amish Adventure - 2nd Edition, Roberta Horton

Appliqué 12 Easy Ways! Elly Sienkiewicz

Basic Seminole Patchwork, Cheryl Greider Bradkin

Beyond the Horizon, Small Landscape Appliqué,
    Valerie Hearder

Buttonhole Stitch Appliqué, Jean Wells

Christmas Traditions From the Heart, (2 Volumes),
    Margaret Peters

Crazy with Cotton, Piecing Together Memories & Themes,
    Diana Leone

Heirloom Machine Quilting, Harriet Hargrave

Impressionist Quilts, Gai Perry

Mastering Machine Appliqué, Harriet Hargrave

The New Sampler Quilt, Diana Leone

Patchwork Quilts Made Easy, Jean Wells   (co-published
    with Rodale Press, Inc.)

Pieces of an American Quilt, Patty McCormick

Quilts for Fabric Lovers, Alex Anderson

Quilts, Quilts, and More Quilts! Diana McClun and
    Laura Nownes

Say It With Quilts, Diana McClun and Laura Nownes

Schoolhouse Appliqué, Reverse Techniques and More,
    Charlotte Patera

Simply Stars, Quilts that Sparkle, Alex Anderson

Small Scale Quiltmaking, Precision, Proportion, and Detail,
    Sally Collins

Tradition with a Twist, Variations on Your Favorite Quilts,
    Blanche Young and Dalene Young Stone

Trapunto by Machine, Hari Walner

A Treasury of Quilt Labels, Susan McKelvey

Willowood, Further Adventures in Buttonhole Stitch Appliqué,
    Jean Wells

For more information write for a free catalog of over
70 titles from:
C&T Publishing
P.O. Box 1456
Lafayette, CA 94549
(1-800-284-1114)